Wetlands

PLANTS IN THEIR HABITATS

Tracey Reeder

PICTURE CREDITS

Cover: Everglades, Florida, USA © David Job/Stone/Getty Images.

Page 1 © David Muench/Corbis/Tranz; page 4, Digital Vision;
page 5 (top) © Cathrine Wessel/Corbis/Tranz; page 5 (bottom left),
Corbis; page 5 (bottom right), Photodisc; page 6 © Patryce Bak/
Stone/Getty Images; page 8 (top) © Robert Pickett/Corbis/Tranz;
page 8 (bottom) © Shuji Kobayashi/Stone+/Getty Images; page 9
© Peter Campbell; page 10 © Peter Adams/The Image Bank/Getty
Images; pages 11–12 © Peter Campbell; page 13 © Arne Hodalic/
Corbis/Tranz; page 14 © Kuljit Kaur; page 15 © David Muench/
Corbis/Tranz; page 16 (top) © Art Wolfe/The Image Bank/Getty
Images; page 16 (bottom left) © Photolibrary; page 16 (bottom
right) © Wolfgang Kaehler/Corbis/Tranz; page 17 (top) © Staffan
Widstrand/Corbis/Tranz; page 17 (bottom) © Jonathan Blair/
Corbis/Tranz; page 18 © Photolibrary; page 21 © Peter Campbell;
page 23 (top) © Macmillan Education Australia; page 23 (bottom)
© Phil Schermeister/Corbis/Tranz; page 24 (left) © Photolibrary;
page 24 (right) © Hal Horwitz/Corbis/Tranz; page 25 (left) © Ted
Dayton/Corbis/Tranz; page 25 (right) © Photolibrary; page 26 (left)
© Photolibrary; page 26 (right), Photodisc;
page 29, Photodisc.

Produced through the worldwide resources of the National
Geographic Society, John M. Fahey, Jr., President and Chief
Executive Officer; Gilbert M. Grosvenor, Chairman of the Board.

PREPARED BY NATIONAL GEOGRAPHIC SCHOOL PUBLISHING
Sheron Long, Chief Executive Officer; Samuel Gesumaria,
President; Steve Mico, Executive Vice President and Publisher;
Francis Downey, Editor in Chief; Richard Easby, Editorial Manager;
Margaret Sidlosky, Director of Design and Illustrations; Jim Hiscott,
Design Manager; Cynthia Olson and Ruth Ann Thompson, Art
Directors; Matt Wascavage, Director of Publishing Services; Lisa
Pergolizzi, Production Manager.

MANUFACTURING AND QUALITY CONTROL
Christopher A. Liedel, Chief Financial Officer; Phillip L. Schlosser,
Vice President; Clifton M. Brown III, Director.

EDITOR
Mary Anne Wengel

PROGRAM CONSULTANTS
Dr. Shirley V. Dickson, National Literacy Consultant; James A.
Shymansky, E. Desmond Lee Professor of Science Education,
University of Missouri-St Louis.

National Geographic Theme Sets program developed by Macmillan
Science and Education Australia Pty Limited.

Published by the National Geographic Society
1145 17th Street N.W.
Washington, D.C. 20036-4688

ISBN: 978-1-4263-5143-3

Printed in China by The Central Printing (Hong Kong) Ltd.
Quarry Bay, Hong Kong
Supplier Code: OCP May 2018
Macmillan Job: 804263
Cengage US PO: 15308030

MEA10_May18_S

Contents

Plants
in Their Habitats

Plants grow almost everywhere on Earth. The places where plants grow are called habitats. A plant gets all it needs to grow from its habitat. There are many different habitats on Earth. Four of these are tropical rain forests, deserts, temperate forests, and wetlands.

 Key Concepts

1. Each part of a plant helps it survive.
2. Adaptations help plants survive in their habitats. There are many different habitats on Earth.
3. Plants and animals depend on one another for survival.

Four Kinds of Habitats

Tropical Rain Forests

Tropical rain forests are good habitats for plants such as tropical hardwood trees.

Deserts

Deserts are good habitats for plants such as cactuses.

In this book you will learn about plants that grow in wetlands such as this one.

Temperate Forests

Temperate forests are good habitats for plants such as red alder trees.

Wetlands

Wetlands are good habitats for plants such as reeds.

Plants of the
Wetlands

Let's take a walk through soggy, boggy wetlands. Your feet sink into the spongy, smelly mud with each step. Look around you in this wet, swampy environment. You will see many plants that float in water. There are grasses, shrubs, and trees. Some plants are dying and rotting in the mud beneath your feet.

Wetlands—Wet all Year Round

Wetlands are low areas of land covered with water. The water stays near or above the surface of the land most of the time. A wetland **habitat** often forms between dry land and lakes or rivers. Wetlands are found in many places on Earth. Many kinds of plants thrive here, including trees and grasses.

Some wetland plants grow under water and others float on the water's surface.

Some wetlands form because the soil in these areas has poor **drainage.** When it rains, the water collects on the ground instead of being absorbed by the soil.

Other wetlands form in boggy areas where underground water is close to Earth's surface. Such wetlands are common in northern Europe and North America.

Wetlands also form when water overflows from rivers and lakes. The wetlands along the Amazon River in South America and the Okavango River in southern Africa formed in this way.

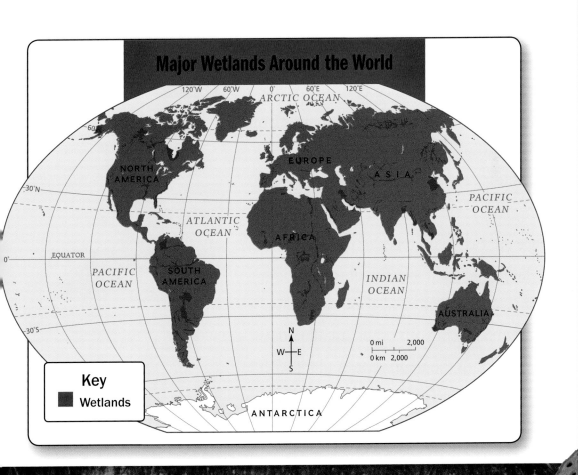

Parts of a Plant

Each plant is made up of many parts, including the roots, stems, leaves, and seeds. Some of these parts are visible, while others are not. No matter how big or how small, each part helps the plant **survive** in its habitat.

survive
to stay alive

Roots You do not see the roots of most plants because they are either submerged in water or buried in the earth. Roots have two important functions that help plants survive. Roots anchor plants firmly in the ground and absorb water and minerals from the soil. All plants need water and minerals to survive.

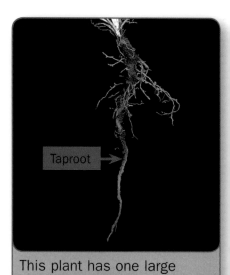

Taproot

This plant has one large taproot.

There are two main types of root systems—the taproot system and the fibrous root system. A plant with a taproot system has a large main root with other smaller roots coming out of the main root. A plant with a fibrous root system has many small roots that are all about the same size.

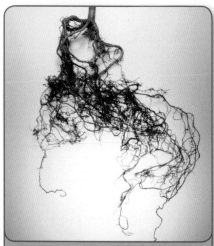

This plant has a fibrous root system.

Stems Stems have two important functions that help a plant survive. The first function is to support the plant. Flowers, fruit, and leaves are all held up by stems. Stems hold up leaves so they can absorb sunlight. Many wetland plants have stems that are, in part, under water. The stems support leaves so that the leaves can receive sunlight.

The second function of stems is to carry food and water to all parts of the plant. Plant stems have two kinds of tubes inside them. Some tubes are called phloem. Phloem carry food from the leaves to other parts of the plant. Other tubes are called xylem. Xylem carry minerals and water from the roots to other parts of the plant.

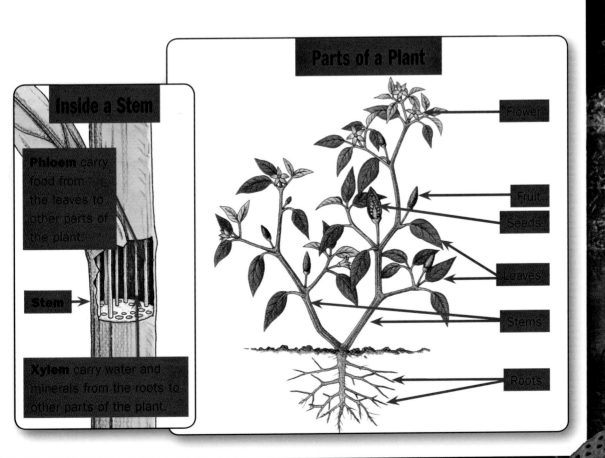

Inside a Stem

Phloem carry food from the leaves to other parts of the plant.

Stem

Xylem carry water and minerals from the roots to other parts of the plant.

Parts of a Plant

Flower

Fruit

Seeds

Leaves

Stems

Roots

Leaves Plant leaves perform an important function. They make food for plants. The food-making process is called **photosynthesis.**

Leaves contain cells called chloroplasts. Chloroplasts are full of a substance that makes the leaves green. This substance is called chlorophyll. During the day, chlorophyll absorbs light energy from the sun. Photosynthesis turns light energy into chemical energy.

During photosynthesis, the leaves split water inside the plant into two gases. These gases are called oxygen and hydrogen. The leaves collect another gas called carbon dioxide from the air. The carbon dioxide combines with hydrogen to make glucose. Plants use glucose as food. The energy in glucose is released in a process called **cellular respiration.** Plants use the glucose the leaves produce to grow. They also use it to reproduce and make repairs. Some glucose particles join together to form starch. Plants store the starch for future use.

During photosynthesis, plants release oxygen into the air. People and animals need the oxygen to breathe.

Large water lily leaves float on the surface of water to absorb sunlight.

Photosynthesis

6. Leaf gives off oxygen.

1. Leaf traps sunlight.

5. Leaf uses hydrogen and carbon dioxide to make a sugar called glucose.

4. Leaf splits water into oxygen and hydrogen.

2. Leaf takes in carbon dioxide from the air.

3. Water travels from the roots to the leaf.

Leaves make food for plants. This process is called photosynthesis.

Seeds Seeds are another important part of a plant. New plants grow from seeds. Inside each seed is an embryo that will grow into a new plant. Seeds also store food to feed the embryo until it grows big enough to make its own food. The food is stored in a cotyledon.

Two kinds of plants produce seeds. These are **gymnosperms** and **angiosperms.** In most gymnosperms, the seeds are in cones. When the cones mature, they open and release the seeds. In angiosperms, seeds are in the flowers or fruit.

Some new plants do not grow from seeds, but from stems that break away. Plants whose stems produce new plants are called **rhizomes.**

Most wetland plants produce new plants either from seeds or from rhizome stems. Reeds are an example of a rhizome. Rice is a wetland plant that grows from seeds.

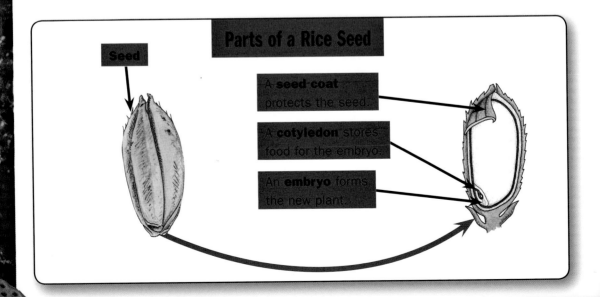

Parts of a Rice Seed

Seed

A **seed coat** protects the seed.

A **cotyledon** stores food for the embryo.

An **embryo** forms the new plant.

Living in a Wetland

An **adaptation** is a feature, or trait, that helps a plant survive in its habitat. Some adaptations help plants survive with little water and sunlight. Other adaptations help plants survive where there are extreme changes in temperature or the ground has few nutrients.

adaptation
a feature that
helps a plant
survive

The roots of plants need oxygen to use the food made in their leaves. Without oxygen, roots cannot conduct cellular respiration. They cannot release the energy from glucose. Plants usually absorb oxygen from the soil through their roots. However, because the soil in wetlands is tightly packed and waterlogged, it does not hold much oxygen. To survive in a wetlands habitat, plants have adaptations to help them grow in wet soil or water.

Mangrove trees have special roots that anchor them to the ground and absorb oxygen from the air.

Living in Water Plants in wetland habitats have many adaptations that allow them to survive. The leaves of most plants have tiny openings, called stomata, on their undersides. Plants absorb carbon dioxide from the air through the stomata. The leaves of many wetland plants have adapted to a wet habitat by developing stomata on their upper sides. Having the stomata on the upper sides allows the leaves to absorb carbon dioxide from the air even when they are floating on water.

Other adaptations help roots get the oxygen they need. Some wetland plants have shallow root systems. These roots spread across the top layer of soil, which is drier and contains more oxygen. Some wetland plants grow their roots out of the water so they can get more oxygen. Other plants have spongy hollow tissue in their stems to help the plant float and to store oxygen when the plant is under water. Other wetland plants have adaptations that allow them to take in oxygen through their leaves. They move the oxygen through their stems to their roots under water.

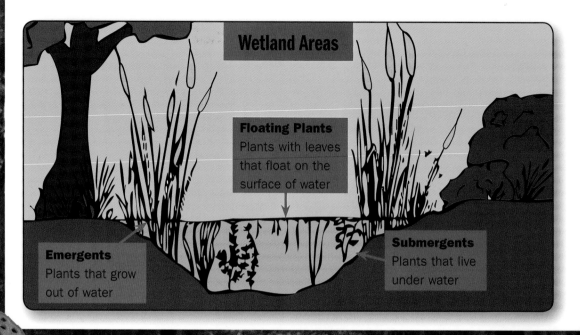

Wetland Areas

Floating Plants
Plants with leaves that float on the surface of water

Emergents
Plants that grow out of water

Submergents
Plants that live under water

Adapting to Poor Soil The soil in most wetlands lacks minerals. Some plants have adapted to get the minerals they need from insects. Plants that get minerals in this way are called carnivorous plants.

The carnivorous pitcher plant gets its name from its long pitcher-shaped leaf. The leaf holds water. The leaf has downward-pointing hairs on the inside. An insect that lands on the leaf may fall into the water in the leaf. The hairs stop it from climbing out and it drowns. The water contains a substance called an enzyme that dissolves the insect. This allows the plant to digest it. Pitcher plants get all the minerals they need from the insects they trap.

Carnivorous plants get their minerals from insects. These plants still make their own food. They use the sun's energy for photosynthesis.

Pitcher plants have adaptations that allow them to catch insects.

Key Concept 3 Plants and animals depend on one another for survival.

Living Together

Many plants and animals live together in a wetland **ecosystem.** They are interdependent, which means they **depend** on one another for their survival.

depend
to need, or rely on, something

Plants and Animals in the Wetlands

Bees and frogs are found in wetland areas. Bees collect nectar from flowers for food. Frogs eat bees.

Bees collect fireweed nectar to make into honey. Bees help pollinate fireweed plants.

Bees are eaten by frogs.

16

Plants Provide Food Plants use the sun's energy to produce food. They are the main producers in an ecosystem. All living things in an ecosystem depend on producers for survival. Plants use energy to grow and reproduce. Energy they do not need is stored. When animals eat plants, this stored energy passes on to them.

Animals that eat only plants are called **herbivores.** Herbivores get their energy directly from plants. Animals that eat other animals are called **carnivores.** Carnivores get their energy indirectly from plants. Energy passing through an ecosystem is called a food chain.

The Nile Delta in Egypt and the Everglades in Florida, United States, are wetlands where hundreds of different kinds of birds and animals live. They feed on the leaves, stems, and fruit of wetland plants. Many migrating birds stop off in wetlands. One billion birds stop off at the Nile Delta each year.

A capybara grazes on plants in a wetland.

A crocodile hunts wetland fish such as mullets.

Animals Spread Pollen and Seeds Many animals help wetland plants reproduce. One way they do this is through **pollination.** Birds and insects feed on the nectar found in flowers. As they feed, they pick up pollen on their bodies. When they fly to another plant, they drop the pollen they have been carrying.

If the pollen falls in a special part of the flower, it **fertilizes** the plant. The flowers then produce seeds from which new plants can grow.

Another way birds help wetland plants survive is by spreading seeds. Birds eat the seeds, along with the other parts of the plant. Seeds that are not completely digested leave the birds' bodies in their droppings. These seeds **germinate** and grow into new plants where they fall.

A bee helps fertilize a wetland daisy by dropping pollen into it.

Some seeds get stuck to a bird's feet when it walks on the muddy ground. As the bird moves about, the seeds fall in different areas. The seeds then germinate and grow into new plants. Geese, ducks, swans, coots, and other wetland birds scatter seeds in this way.

Think About the **Key Concepts**

Think about what you read. Think about the pictures and diagrams. Use these to answer the questions. Share what you think with others.

1. How do the different parts of a plant help it survive?

2. What happens during photosynthesis?

3. What adaptations help plants survive?

4. How do animals help plants survive?

Labeled Diagram

Diagrams are pictures that show information.
You can learn new ideas without having to read many words. Diagrams use pictures and words to explain ideas.

There are different kinds of diagrams.
This diagram of a lotus plant is a **labeled diagram.** A labeled diagram is a picture that shows the parts of something. It can give information about each part. Look back at the diagram on page 9. It is a labeled diagram of the parts of a plant.

How to Read a Diagram

1. **Read the title.**
   The title tells you what the diagram is about.

2. **Read the labels.**
   The labels name the parts of the diagram. They may also give information about the parts.

3. **Study the diagram.**
   Use the labels to help you understand the diagram.

4. **Think about what you learned.**
   Decide what new information you learned from the diagram.

A Lotus Plant

Lotus seeds form in lotus pods.

Lotus flowers can be white or pink.

20 centimeters (8 inches) in height

The leaves emerge from the water on long stems.

What Have You Learned?

Read the diagram by following the steps on page 20. Write down all the things you have learned about the lotus plant. Share the things you have learned with a classmate. Compare what you learned. What is the same? What is different?

Reference Sources

The purpose of reference sources is to inform. Reference sources can take many forms.

You use different reference sources for different purposes. For example, if you want to know how to spell *cranberry*, use a dictionary. But if you want to know facts about a cranberry plant, use an **encyclopedia.**

You do not read a reference source from beginning to end. You read only the parts that cover topics you want to learn about.

Encyclopedia
of Wetland Plants

This sample shows seven encyclopedia entries.
Encyclopedia entries give basic facts about many
topics. All the entries in this encyclopedia are
about wetland plants.

Cattail

- found in most wetland areas
- uses: food, weaving, building
- parts used: roots, leaves

Title names the topic.

List gives facts about the topic.

Text gives important information.

Cattail reeds have swordlike leaves
and a stalk with a long, brown spike at
the end. When the plant is pollinated,
the brown spike gets fluffy with seeds.
These seeds blow away to become new
plants. Cattails grow in dense groups.

Birds build their nests among cattails,
and fish hide under them in the water.
People peel and cook the root of the
cattail. They also pound it into flour.
People make the leaves into baskets,
mats, and building materials.

Photographs help you
picture what you are reading.

Captions give more information. ▲ Cattails are grasslike plants found
in wetlands.

Cranberry

- found in North America
- uses: food, dye
- part used: fruit

The cranberry is a shrub that grows in bogs. It grows to 20 centimeters (8 inches) high. It has thin, wiry stems that have small evergreen leaves. The berries start out white and turn a bright red when ripe.

Native Americans used the berries for food, medicine, and fabric dyes. Today, people grow cranberries to eat fresh or dried. They use cranberries to make sauce, jelly, and juice.

▲ Cranberries grow on low-lying vines, or stems, along the ground.

Goldthread

- found in North America
- uses: medicine, dye
- part used: roots

Goldthread grows in cool and moist bogs. It has star-shaped white flowers and waxy leaves. The roots are a golden yellow. It does not grow higher than 15 centimeters (6 inches).

Native Americans chewed goldthread roots to treat mouth sores. They also made dye from the roots and used it to color quills, feathers, and animal skins. People used goldthread to make an eyewash to soothe sore eyes. Today, people use it to soothe swellings and kill bacteria.

▲ Goldthread roots are collected in fall after the plant has flowered.

Lotus

- found in Asia
- use: food
- parts used: roots, seeds

The lotus is a member of the water lily family. The root grows under water. From this root, the leaves, flowers, and seed heads grow and emerge from the water.

The root and seeds of the lotus can be cooked. They are delicious roasted, fried, boiled, pickled, or candied. In the Buddhist religion, the lotus symbolizes people having their feet in the mud but rising to a pure and graceful state.

Marshmallow

- found in Europe and North America
- uses: food, medicine
- parts used: sap, leaves

The marshmallow is a herb. It grows to 120 centimeters (47 inches) high. It grows well in salt marshes, or on riverbanks and lake edges.

People originally combined the sap of the marshmallow plant with sugar and flavors to make marshmallow candy. Today, candy manufacturers use gelatin instead of marshmallow sap. The marshmallow plant contains a thick, gooey substance that can soothe sore throats. People also drink marshmallow tea.

▲ Lotus leaves and flowers sometimes float on the surface of water.

▲ Marshmallows get their name from the marshy places they grow.

Peat Moss

- found in most wetland areas
- use: wound dressing
- part used: leaves

Peat moss forms soft, spongy mats on the surface of bogs. Peat mosses are red, brown, yellow, and green in color.

Peat moss absorbs fluid better than cotton. During World War I, people used it to dress wounds. Today, manufacturers of health care products use it to make surgical dressings. Gardeners spread peat moss on the ground around delicate plants such as orchids. Peat moss keeps the plants from drying out in hot weather.

Rice

- found in Asia, Africa, Europe, South America, and North America
- use: food
- part used: seeds

Rice is a grass. The rice plant has long, narrow leaves and several hollow stems. Seed heads filled with rice grains grow at the ends of the tall stems.

Rice grows best in shallow water, so people flood fields with water to grow rice. Rice is the world's second most important food crop and provides food for more than half of the world's people.

▲ Peat mosses absorb and store water in their stems and leaves.

▲ Farmers flood their fields with water to create wetlands for rice plants.

Apply the **Key Concepts**

Key Concept 1 Each part of a plant helps it survive.

Activity

Choose a plant from a wetland and draw it. Label the parts of the plant that help it survive. Write captions that explain how the parts of the plant help it survive.

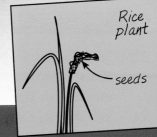

Rice plant

seeds

Key Concept 2 Adaptations help plants survive in their habitats. There are many different habitats on Earth.

Activity

Create a two-column chart that explains how plants adapt to the wetland habitat. Label one column "Habitat Conditions" and the other column "Plant Adaptations."

Habitat Conditions	Plant Adaptations

Key Concept 3 Plants and animals depend on one another for survival.

Activity

Plants and animals help one another survive. List three plant and animal pairs that depend on each other in a wetland. Explain how each helps the other.

Plant and Animal Pairs

1.

2.

3.

Create
Your Own
Encyclopedia

Many plants live in wetlands. You have read about some of them. Now it is time to find out about more of them. Get ready to do some research. Then make a book about wetland plants. You can work with others to make a group book.

1. Study the Model

Look back at pages 23–26. Pick one plant you think is interesting. Now look closely at the entry for that plant. What facts are included? Do these tell about different parts of the plant? How does it reproduce? How does it adapt to the wetland habitat? These are the kinds of facts you might want to include in your entry.

Encyclopedia Entries
- Each entry is about one person, place, or thing.
- Use a title to say what the entry is about.
- Use pictures with labels to show what things look like.
- Include important facts.

2. Choose Your Topic

You cannot write about what you do not know. Start by looking through books about wetland plants. Look at the pictures. Read about plants that look interesting. For each plant, ask yourself:
- What is special about this plant?
- What facts are important?
- Does the picture show what the plant looks like?

List the plants that you think are interesting. Then pick the one you would like to learn more about.

3. Research Your Topic

Question

Ask yourself what you want to know. Make a list of questions. Use this list to guide your research. To find facts about your plant, look through books. Look on the Internet.

Take Notes

Keep track of what you find out. Take notes. Use a chart to help you sort your notes. Make copies of pictures you might want to use.

Arrowhead

1. What does it look like?

2. Where does it grow?

3. How do people use it?

4.

4. Write a Draft

Look over the facts you found. Now look back at one of the entries on pages 23–26. Use it as a model for writing about your plant. Be sure to use the important facts you collected. Also include any interesting or weird facts about your plant.

5. Revise and Edit

Read your draft. What do you like? What would you like to change? Make these changes. Then read your draft again. This time, fix any mistakes. Look for words that are misspelled. Be sure each sentence starts with a capital letter.

Create Your Own Book

Now you can share your work. Get together with others to make a class book. Follow the steps below.

How to Make a Book

1. **Check that each entry has a title.**
   Check that the title names the plant in the entry.
2. **Include a photo or drawing for each entry.**
   Use a photo or draw a picture of your plant.
3. **Add captions to pictures.**
   Captions and labels tell what pictures are about.
4. **Organize the entries alphabetically.**
   Put each entry in alphabetical order.
5. **Number the pages.**
   Add the page number for each page.
6. **Prepare a table of contents.**
   Look at the table of contents in this book. Now make one for your book.
7. **Make a cover.**
   Talk with your group about what you want on your cover. Choose pictures and decide on a title. Then make your cover.
8. **Now bind the pages together.**
   You can staple the pages together. Or you can punch holes on the left side and tie the pages together with yarn.

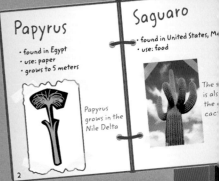

Papyrus
- found in Egypt
- use: paper
- grows to 5 meters

Papyrus grows in the Nile Delta

2

Saguaro
- found in United States, M
- use: food

The s is als the cac

Plant Encyclopedia

Glossary

adaptation – a feature that helps a plant survive

angiosperms – a group of plants that have seeds covered with fruit

carnivores – animals that eat only meat

cellular respiration – the process by which plants breathe

depend – to need, or rely on, something

drainage – way of draining, or removing, water

ecosystem – a community of plants and animals living together in an area

fertilizes – makes a plant fertile and able to produce seeds

germinate – to sprout

gymnosperms – a group of plants that have seeds that are uncovered

habitat – a place where a plant or animal usually lives in nature

herbivores – animals that eat only plants

photosynthesis – the process by which plants make food

pollination – transferring pollen to enable a plant to produce seeds

rhizomes – stems from which new plants grow

survive – to stay alive

Index